USING AN INHALER

BookLife
freedom
Readers

with the

HUMAN BODY HELPERS

BY HARRIET BRUNDLE

BookLife
PUBLISHING

©2022
BookLife Publishing Ltd.
King's Lynn
Norfolk PE30 4LS

A catalogue record for this book is available from the British Library.

ISBN: 978-1-80155-133-5

Written by:
Harriet Brundle

Edited by:
Kirsty Holmes

Designed by:
Danielle Rippengill

All facts, statistics, web addresses and URLs in this book were verified as valid and accurate at time of writing. No responsibility for any changes to external websites or references can be accepted by either the author or publisher.

IMAGE CREDITS

All images are courtesy of Shutterstock.com, unless otherwise specified. With thanks to Getty Images, Thinkstock Photo and iStockphoto.
Front Cover & 1 – Beatriz Gascon J, NikaMooni, LOVE YOU. Larry – Beatriz Gascon J. Izzy – LOVE YOU. 2 – EstherQueen999, Nik Symkin. 5 & 6 – Teerapol24. 6 – Igdeeva Alena. 12 – Nik Symkin. 16 – Teerapol24. 17 – Igdeeva Alena. 19 – K-D-uk. 20 – Studio Barcelona. 21 – EstherQueen999. 22 – Sashatigar.

CONTENTS

YOUR LUNGS

Your lungs are a very important organ in your body that allow you to breathe. They have tubes coming out of them. These lead to your windpipe, which joins your lungs to your throat.

Hi, I'm Larry Lung! I'm one half of your lungs.

OXYGEN AND OTHER GASES

When you breathe in, your lungs fill up with many gases, including oxygen. As you breathe out, your lungs get rid of waste gases, including carbon dioxide. If you put your hand on your chest and breathe in, you can feel your lungs in action.

WHAT IS ASTHMA?

Asthma is a disease which makes breathing difficult. With asthma, the tubes which carry air in and out of your lungs can become inflamed. The muscles around the tubes tighten, making the tubes narrower. Asthma can also make your lungs make extra mucus.

Asthma can make you feel very short of breath, have a cough or wheeze. Lots of different things can cause your airways to tighten. These include animal hair, cold air and doing exercise.

WHAT IS AN INHALER?

An inhaler is a small device which helps you to breathe medicine into your lungs. You might need to use inhalers if you have asthma, especially if you have asthma attacks.

An asthma attack happens when your asthma suddenly gets much worse. You may feel like you cannot breathe, your chest may feel very tight or you may have a cough. It is important to tell an adult as soon you feel unwell.

Reliever inhalers are usually blue. They work very quickly to open up your airways to make you feel better and help you breathe.

You may also need a preventer inhaler, which helps to protect your airways. They are usually brown and can reduce the symptoms of your asthma. If used correctly, a preventer inhaler can lower the risk of you having an asthma attack.

WHAT HAPPENS WHEN YOU VISIT THE DOCTOR?

If you feel any of the symptoms of asthma, it is important that you tell an adult. You will need to go and see the doctor, who will ask you a few questions about how you are feeling.

spirometer results

1 2 3
4 5 6
7 8 9 0

start stop

DOCTOR

The doctor may ask you to blow into special machines that can tell them all sorts of information about your lungs. A doctor will then prescribe an inhaler if they think you need it.

HOW DO I USE
MY INHALER?

Take off the cap and check there is nothing in the mouthpiece. Shake your inhaler, stand or sit straight and breathe out. Place your mouth around the mouthpiece and, as you slowly breathe in, press the top once.

PRESS HERE

CAP

MOUTHPIECE

Keep breathing in but take your inhaler out of your mouth. Keep your lips closed and hold your breath for as long as you comfortably can. Breathe out away from your inhaler. It might take a few practices to get it right.

HOW DO INHALERS WORK?

Each puff of air that comes out of your inhaler has medicine in it which helps your asthma. As you breathe it in, the medicine goes straight to your lungs. You should only use an inhaler when you feel the symptoms of asthma.

MEDICINE

The medicine relaxes the muscles around your airways, which makes the airways widen. This means you can breathe more easily, and the symptoms of asthma are lessened.

BEFORE

AFTER

WHAT TO EXPECT

Once you have learnt how to use your inhaler correctly, you should find that your inhaler helps you to feel much better.

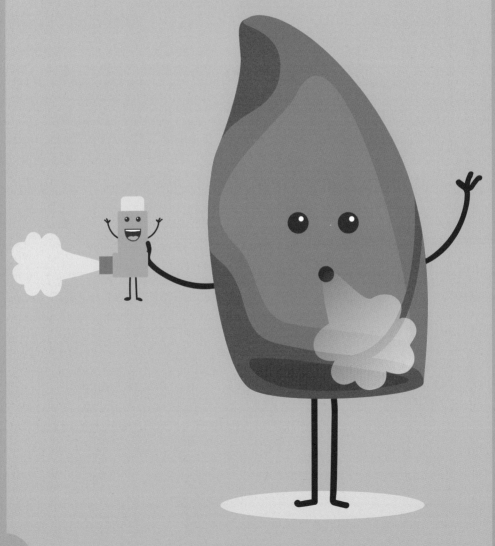

If you find it hard to use your inhaler, you may be able to use a spacer with it. This is a large tube that you can attach to your inhaler. It holds the medicine so you can breathe it in more easily. The doctor or pharmacist can show you how to use one.

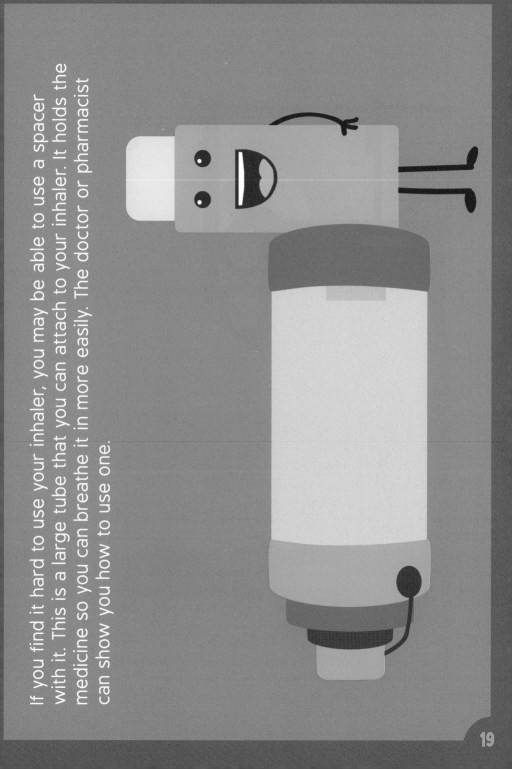

DOS AND DON'TS

Do try to live a healthy lifestyle by eating healthily and exercising if you feel like you can. Do make sure you do a few test sprays before using your inhaler if you have not used it for a few days, or if it is new.

Do speak to your doctor and read any instructions before you use your inhaler for the first time to be sure that you are using it correctly. Do not use your inhaler more or less than you are supposed to.

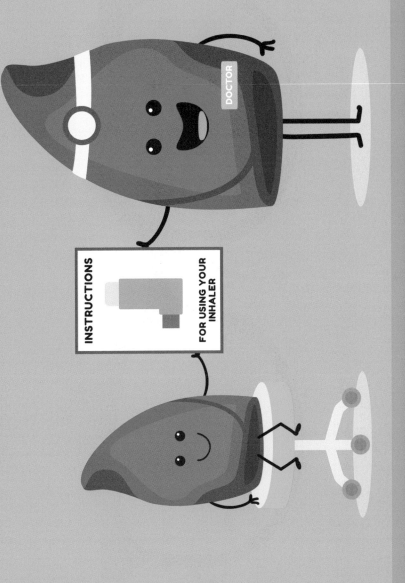

LIFE AFTER
INHALERS

For some children, asthma can get much better as they get older. It can even go away completely. This means they no longer need an inhaler or feel any symptoms of asthma.

For others, their asthma might carry on throughout their lives. With the right treatment, asthma can be kept under control so it does not affect day-to-day life too much.

QUESTIONS

1: What do the lungs help you do?

2: What does asthma do?
   a) Makes it harder to breathe
   b) Makes it easier to breathe
   c) It doesn't do anything

3: Usually, what colour is a reliever inhaler?

4: How do you use an inhaler?

5: Name one thing you shouldn't do with an inhaler.

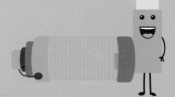